Advance Forex Trading Strategies

Strategies For Every Trading

George Morgan

Copyright©2022 George Morgan
All Right Reserve

- Advanced Forex Trading Strategies 5
- Day Trading Strategies 6
- 60 Seconds Scalping Strategy 13
- Fading Trading Strategy 16
- Pivot Point Trading Strategy 18
- Pivot Point in the Forex Market 22
- Momentum Trading Strategy 25
- Carry Trade Strategy 29
- Hedging Strategy 33
- Basket Trading Strategy 38
- Buy and Hold Strategy 40
- Pair/Spread Trading Strategy 43
- Swing Trading Strategy 47
- Trading Order Types Strategy 50
- Algorithmic Trading Strategies 57

Introduction

Advance Trading Strategies, outlines every aspect of a practical trading plan from exit to entry. The result is a complete approach to trading that will allow you to trade confidently in a variety of markets and time frames. Written with the serious trader in mind, this reliable resource details a proven approach to analyzing market behavior, identifying profitable trade setups, and executing and managing trades.

Trading today's markets including Forex, stocks and futures can be a challenging and difficult endeavor. But it is possible to achieve consistent success in this field, if you're prepared to learn a complete trading strategy from entry to exit.

With this book as your guide, you'll quickly learn how to manage a trade until it's completely closed out. As you become familiar with the proven strategies and profitable trades techniques taught. With Advanced Trading Strategies, you'll also come to understand the type of market data you can use to make specific trade decisions and how to execute those decisions from start to finish

While the ideas found here are essential to trading success, the best way to learn is by example, you'll see how to apply these strategies taught throughout the book to markets around the world.

Advances Trading Strategies details a practical approach to analyzing market behavior, identifying profitable trade setups, and executing and managing trades which will allow you to both preserve and grow your capital.

If you're looking to make the most of your time in today's markets, look no further than Advance Trading Strategy.

Advanced Forex Trading Strategies

Utilizing and creating trading strategies generally relies upon understanding your strength and weaknesses. For one to be very profitable in trade, its advisable to find the most ideal way of trading that suits your type of person, because there is no direct, laid down principle or best approach to trading; the correct way for others may not be the best way for you.

Forex trading strategies can be created by following famous trading styles which can be any of the following;

1. Algorithmic trading
2. Order trading
3. Buy and hold strategy
4. Day trading
5. Hedging
6. Spread Trading
7. Swing trading
8. Portfolio trading
9. Carry trading

Beneath you can find out about each trading style and characterize whats work for you.

Day Trading Strategies

Focus points
- Keep feelings under control
- Day trading requires consistent consideration and stress obstruction.
- To prevail in day trading, traders strategies ought to be founded on profound technical analysis utilizing charts, pointers and models to anticipate future price developments.

Day Trading Strategies
This is a momentary or 24 hours trading strategy that's has to do with buying and selling of financial instrument under 24 hours, so as to benefit from little developments of price. Day traders should be ceaselessly engaged, since market sectors, for example, the oil market can move unexpectedly in a short term. Consequently these techniques are especially powerful in volatile markets.

Below are some well known best day trading strategy:
Day trading strategies are fundamental if a trader has any desire to profit from incessant and little price variances. A compelling strategies ought to be founded on profound technical analysis utilizing chart, pointers and models to foresee future price developments.
Below we would consider the most widely recognized day trading strategies;

- **Scalp Trading Strategy**

Scalp strategy depends on opening and shutting off numerous positions on at least one Forex pairs throughout the day, usually in seconds or minutes during the course of a trend.
Traders ought to constantly put in consideration the market's liquidity and instability prior to taking on a forex scalping strategy. Utilizing leverage is a significant part while utilizing a scalping strategy- it helps to increasing the profits.

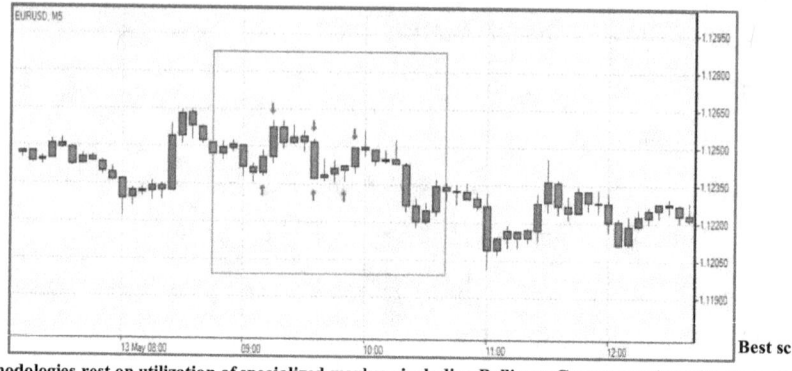

Best scalping methodologies rest on utilization of specialized markers including Bollinger Groups, moving midpoints, the stochastic oscillator, parabolic SAR and RSI.

Important points

- ✓ **Scalping is not a long-term strategy, the main objective is to create profit out of little price developments.**
- ✓ **Scalpers typically need a bigger deposit in order to have the option to deal with how much leverage they need to use to make short and little trade to work.**
- ✓ **Scalpers shouldn't risk beyond what they can bear to lose.**

Scalping in Forex Trading

Forex Scalping strategy is not a long term trading strategy, the objective is to create gain out of small price developments. A good forex scalping methodologies include utilizing leveraged trading. This leverage make it possible for traders to get capital from a broker so as to acquire more openness to the Forex market, just using a little level of the full resource value as a deposit. Regardless of the fact that this strategy increases ones profit it has a high tendency of also multiplying losses one the market moves against you. Hence, forex scalpers are expected to watch out for the market for any changes no matter how little.

Yet, before everything, Below are few significant things traders has to be aware of:

- ◆ **Always trade the most liquid pairs** - USD/CHF, GBP/USD, USD/JPY and EUR/USD these currency pairs are the most liquid currency pairs so they offer the most secure spreads since they will generally have the most elevated trading volume. Traders need to search for most impenetrable spreads, since they will enter the market frequently.
- ◆ **Spreads and Transaction Expenses** - Each trade has its own transaction costs, scalping can bring about additional expenses than benefits.
- ◆ **Traders can be Confused by News Report** - Market instability is broadly impacted by news declarations and reports like macroeconomics or Gross domestic product information, since brokers normally could rush to make a fast buck - causing chain response.
- ◆ **Trading during the most active times** - from 2:00 am to 4:00 am and from 8:00 am to 12:00 early afternoon Eastern Time.
- ◆ **Risk Control** - Because of the little benefits from scalping, traders utilize bigger leverage than expected. Yes leverage can increase benefits, and yet it can likewise prompt critical losses. So in the event that the a trader anticipate utilizing a higher leverage ratio, a risk control management is significant.

Traders ought to likewise focus on their risk/reward ratio. This is on the grounds that traders will frequently get halted in most of situations where the loop between their take benefit and stop misfortune levels are slim.

Best Scalping Technique

As earlier referenced, the best scalping techniques rest on the utilization of technical indicators including the **Stochastic Oscillator, parabolic SAR and RSI Bollinger Bands and Moving Averages.**

Stochastic oscillator - is a force indicator looking at a specific closing cost of a security to a scope of its costs over a specific timeframe. Indicators is well known for producing overbought and oversold signals.

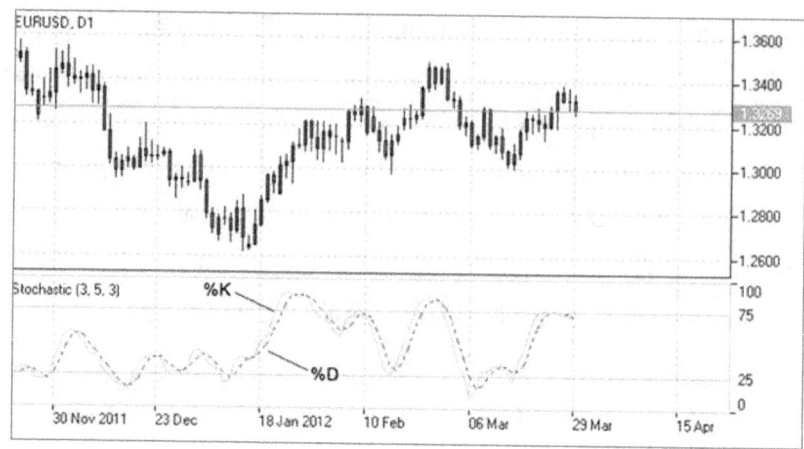

The Stochastic Oscillator chart as a rule comprises of two lines: one addresses the genuine worth of the oscillator for every session, and the other addresses its three-day straightforward moving average. Since cost is accepted to be following force, the intersection of these two lines is viewed as a sign that a reversal might be underway, as it shows an enormous change in force from one day to another.

The difference between the Stochastic Oscillator and the trending price activity is additionally viewed as a significant reversal signal. For instance, when a bearish trends makes a fresh lower low, yet the oscillator makes a higher low, it very well may be a pointer that bearish force is running out and a bullish reversal is blending. As seen in the chart above.

Parabolic stop and reverse (SAR) - is utilized to decide the price movement of an asset, as well as cause to notice when the price movement is changing direction. On the chart below shown as red spots above or underneath the market price.

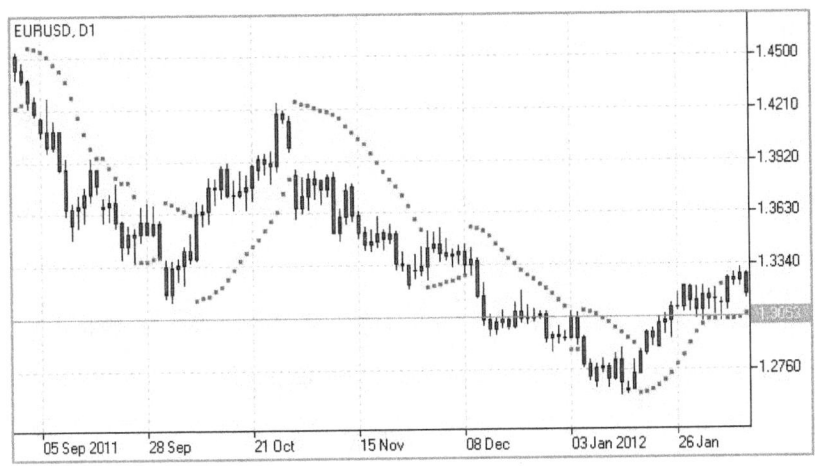

A point beneath the price is viewed as a bullish sign, as well as the other way around - a point over the price is utilized to represent that bearish force is in charge and that it is probably going to remain downtrend. At the point when the sots are exchanged, it shows that there is a potential shift in the direction of the price. For instance, in the event that the sports are over the price when they turn over beneath the price, this could flag a further increase in price.

Now as the share price rises, the spots will likewise rise, gradually from the outset, and afterward picking up speed and advancing rapidly alongside the trend. SAR begins to move a little quicker as the trend creates, and soon the points meets up with the price.

Relative strength index (RSI) - is a force indicator, utilizes a scope of somewhere in the range of zero and 100 to evaluate whether the market's ongoing direction may be close to reverse. It utilizes levels of support and resistance- set at 30 and 70 individually - to recognize when the market's pattern may be going to take a different path.

At the point when the RSI transcends 70, it most likely shows that the market is overbought and a trader might open a short position. Assuming the RSI falls under 30, it likely shows that the market is oversold and a trader ought to open a long position.

Scalpers ought to execute these pointers in their techniques and a big part of the work is finished.

Bollinger Bands: is utilized to demonstrate areas of market instability. They depend on simple moving average (SMA) with a standard deviation set above and underneath to show how unpredictable a market may be. Traders accept that more wider standard deviations show expanded unpredictability in as well as the other way around, on the off chance that the bands are thin it could imply that the market is steady.

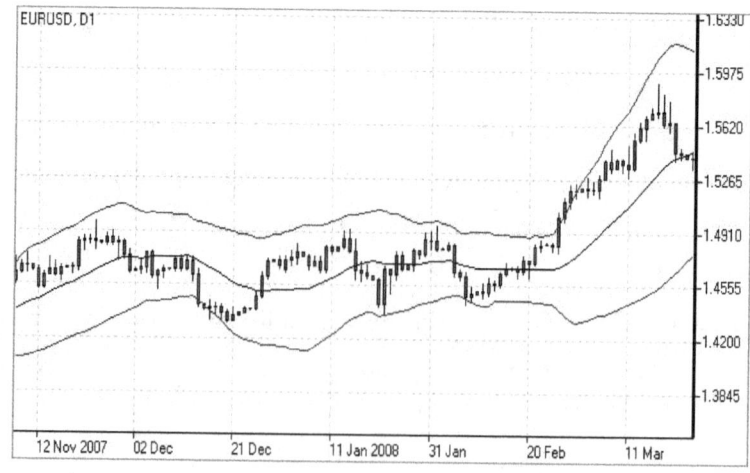

The Bollinger Bands can be partitioned into two groups of importance:
1. **Breakouts** - Any breakout above or underneath the bands is a significant event..
2. **The Squeeze**- int the event that the bands draw nearer together, restricting the moving average, it is known as a squeeze. A squeeze flags a time of low unpredictability and is viewed as a likely indication of future uplifted volatility and conceivable trading potential. On the other hand, the more extensive the bands move, the higher the probability of a decline in volatility and the higher the probability of leaving an trade.

Moving Average (MA) - A moving normal is a numerical equation that assists with spotting arising and normal trends in markets, represented as a solitary line showing an average. The justification for working out the moving average of a stock is to assist with streamlining the price information by making a continually updated average price.

Simple moving average (SMA) - **s** determined by taking the arithmetic mean of a given set of values over a predefined timeframe.

Exponential moving averagel (EMA) - gives more weight to recent costs, making it more receptive to new data. Traders should initially compute (SMA) throughout a specific time span. Then, they need to work out the multiplier for weighting the EMA which - [2/(selected time span + 1)].

So for instance, for a 45 - day moving average, the multiplier would be [2/(45+1)]= 0.0435. Then traders ought to utilize the smoothing factor joined with the past EMA to arrive at the ongoing value.

60 Seconds Scalping Strategy

Due to the fact that scalpers profits are low, they need to open many trades over the course of the day and close them in couple of seconds or minutes.
This strategy depends on pattern following which assists with bringing to the minimum misleading signs. However it doesn't preclude the need of appropriate risk control management connected to it.

Unpredictable market is a vital part of scalping strategy; traders can bring in money based on price variances. Utilizing the New York-London session cross-over; it's the point at which the market is the most unpredictable - during those couple of hours price are low and liquidity is high.

For this technique to be effective traders will require one oscillator and two moving midpoints.

- **Time span: 60 seconds;**
- **Favored session: London, New York - high volatility.**
- **Instruments: any cash pair;**
- **Pointers: Stochastic 5, 3, 3 and 50 EMA, 100 EMA;**

Both moving average are utilized to distinguish the latest trend in the 60 seconds time frame. 100 EMA is utilized to calculate the average cost for the past 100 minutes and the 50 EMA for the past 50 minutes. 50 EMA responds on price developments more rapidly than 100 EMA, so it's quicker, the two of them give a decent comprehension of a trend.

At the point when the 50-time frame EMA crosses over the 100-time frame EMA, it implies that average price are beginning to rise which is a bullish sign. Likewise, when a cross of the 50-time frame EMA underneath the 100-period EMA it's a sign that average costs begin to drop and that is a bearish sign. When a short term trend is characterized traders ought to sit tight for a pullback to the moving average. It's significant in light of the fact that prices will generally get back to their mean value after a solid up-or down-move. Sitting tight for pullbacks keeps traders from falling into misleading signs and misfortunes. The last filter Stochastic pointer will assist traders with separating high probability traders. This pointer fluctuates somewhere in the range of 0 and 100 values, contingent upon the strength of latest price developments. At the point when the value is over 80, it implies that the new up-move was solid and the market is overbought, consequently the down-move is normal, when the value is under 20, the market is oversold, up move is supposed to occur.

Advantages Of Stock Scalping
- Don't bother following fundamentals
- Can be utilized in the event that the market is fluctuating.
- Can be entirely productive whenever executed unequivocally and with a severe exit strategy and effective risk control management.
- Numerous chances to leverage little changes in the price of a stock
- Market risk involved is very little.
- Can without much of a stretch be robotized inside the trading system.

Disadvantages Of Stock Scalping
- Requires more leverage to enable profit (The bigger the leverage the bigger the profit same as the loss)
- High exchange fee.
- It is tedious strategy and requires a lot of concentration

Forex Scalping Strategy In a Nut Shell
Obviously, the Forex market is huge and unstable; however we have technical analysis that gives a practical strategy for trading this market. Scalping is likewise viewed as a suitable strategy for the Forex traders. Be that as it may, forex scalpers for the most part need a bigger deposit to have the option to deal with how much leverage they need to use to make short and little traders to work. Scalping requires concentration and speed and it's indispensable if traders have any desire to find success. So in the event that traders like the activity and really like to zero in on 60 or 120 seconds charts, then scalping is exactly what was needed. To summarize; On the off chance that a trader has high resilience to losses and a disposition to respond rapidly then scalping is a decent counterpart for him/her.

Fading Trading Strategy

Fading strategy is unsafe and normally best when done by proficient expert traders, who comprehends technical analysis well and are knowledgeable about deciphering charts. Don't forget that fading the market isn't ideal for everybody. Fading strategy It's a contradicting trading procedure, where traders trade against the prevailing trend..

This strategy is often used in forex when there is a major economic news released.

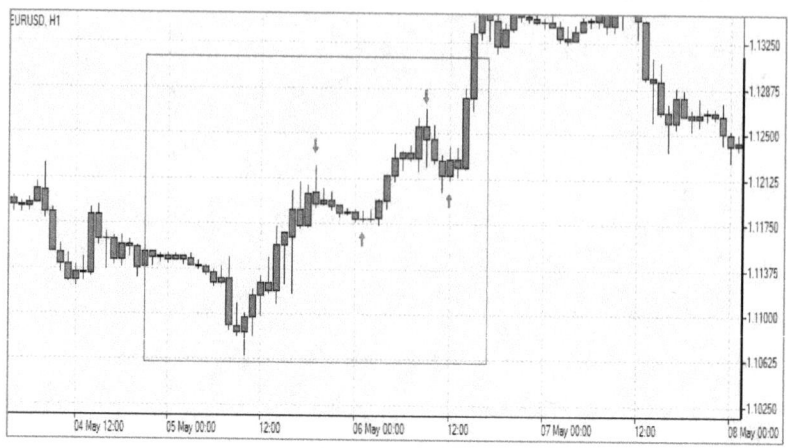

Traders who utilize this strategy are selling when the costs are rising and purchasing when it is falling. The thought behind this strategy is that the market has proactively considered all the data, and the later phases of the trend are predominantly upheld by those traders who respond leisurely, which will improve the probability of a trend inversion.

For instance, antagonist financial investors could purchase stocks after an organization advises investors and the public that its profit results won't meet analyst assumptions. They explains their choice for buying with the market overreach.

Fading is by large an unpredictable strategy that will create critical transient benefits. This doesn't need complicated analysis, yet the risk of a trend continuation is unavoidably present.

Remember that fading trading strategy implies that a traders purchases when the market is selling and sells when the market is purchasing. Despite the fact that there is a chance for enormous momentary benefits with a fade strategy, a proficient fade trader won't participate in this strategy aimlessly. There is a great tendency to experience huge loss on the off chance that a trend proceeds, however assuming that a fade trader effectively distinguishes when a security is moving excessively far from its actual value, the trader will gain by the reversal..

When there is a lot of volatility in the market a fading strategy is most effective, as there will be possibly productive remedies. While utilizing this strategy traders will hang tight for key statistics information release; income reports, loan fees or deals projections. This strategy can be utilized on stocks, however it is more reasonable for Forex markets, in light of the fact that after reports are released there are critical fluctuations of currencies.

Novice traders ought to abstain from fade trading. Utilizing this strategy involves a ton of risk and needs the support of a specialist. Trader ought to painstakingly consider there financial situations and resistance to risk prior to taking huge fade positions. Execution of risk management is significant too, in a nutshell, proper research and risk management is a foundation for an effective trading strategy.

Pivot Point Trading Strategy

This trading strategy is a traders closest companion with regards to distinguishing levels to develop an inclination, recognize potential benefit targets and stop loss for a trade. Traders utilized pivot points on stock and commodity trades. The pivot point are calculated in light of the highs, lows and close prices of past exchanging sessions and are utilized to anticipate support and resistance levels in the current or forthcoming session. Support and resistance levels can be utilized by traders to decide when to take profit or stop loss as well as entry and exit point.

Types of Pivot Point Strategy
- **Bounce Strategy**
- **Intraday Strategy**
- **Trend Trading Strategy**
- **Reversal Trading Strategy**

Bounce Strategy

Here the philosophy is that assuming the price is over the pivot point, the market opinion is bullish. In the event that the price is beneath the pivot point, the market opinion is bearish. The pivot point exploits market sentiment, either by buying or selling once the price retraces backwards to the pivot point, which is a significant flat support or resistance level.

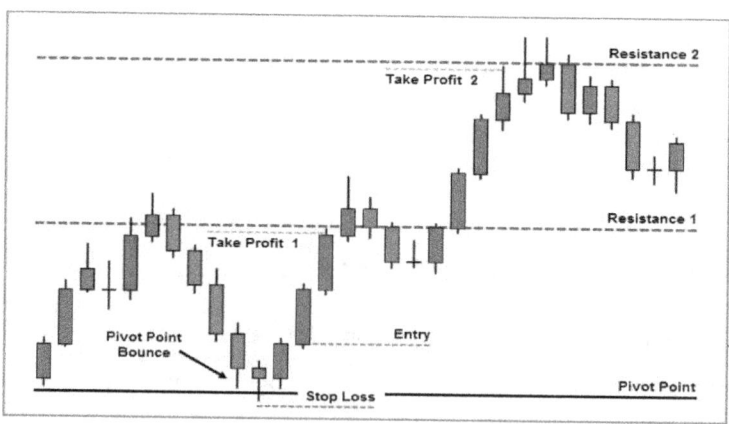

Intraday Strategy

This strategy are generally utilized by daily traders, on 10 minutes, 15minutes and 60 minutes charts. No matter what the time span utilized, the pivot levels stay equivalent as they depend on a numerical formula for the earlier day's high, low and close. Chart time spans just show price activity detail happening within the pivot point pointers (indicators) levels. Let's take a look at an example so you can visualize this. Here's a 15-minute chart of GBP/USD.

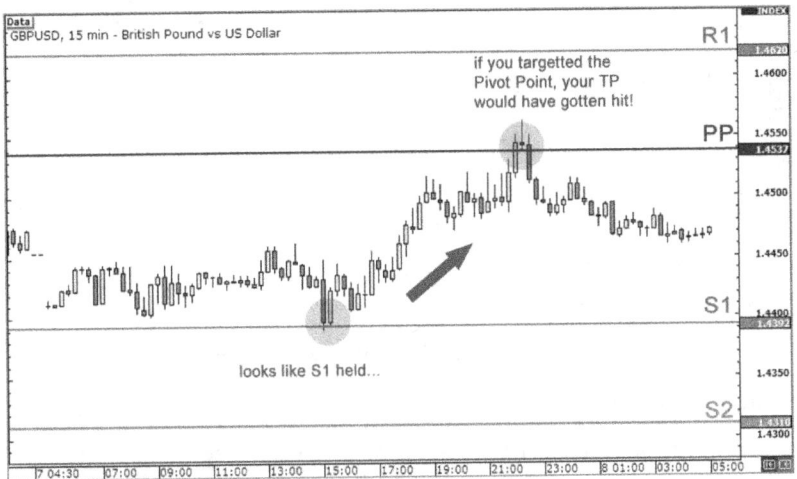

Trend Trading Strategy

Pivot points can also be used for trend trading. It is believed that after the prices has picked the direction in light of the pivot point, the trader can exploit amendments at noticeable levels. In the event that cost convincingly gets through the first support or resistance level an pulls back, at that point the trader can sell or buy on the bounce off that level.

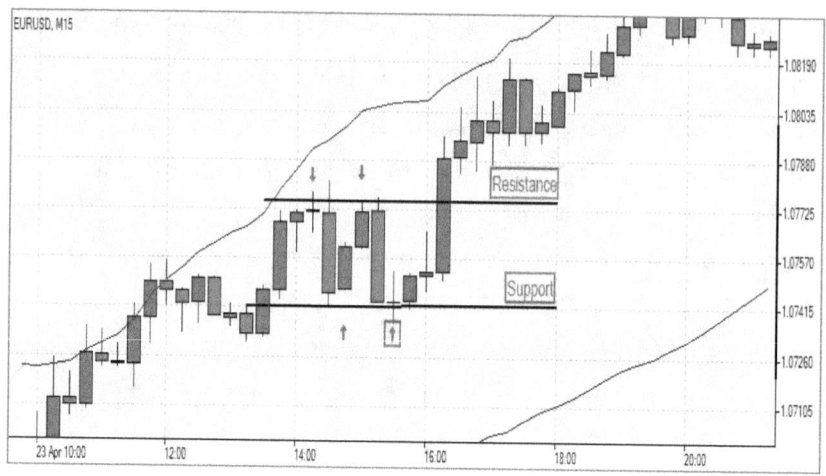

Reversal Strategy

In the reversal strategy the support and resistance levels determined through pivot point can be utilized for reversal exchanges also. In the event that price is dialing back close to the second or third support and resistance levels it's a decent spot to trade (buy and sell) separately. This is in light that at support and resistance levels 1 and 2, the price is probably going to extend.

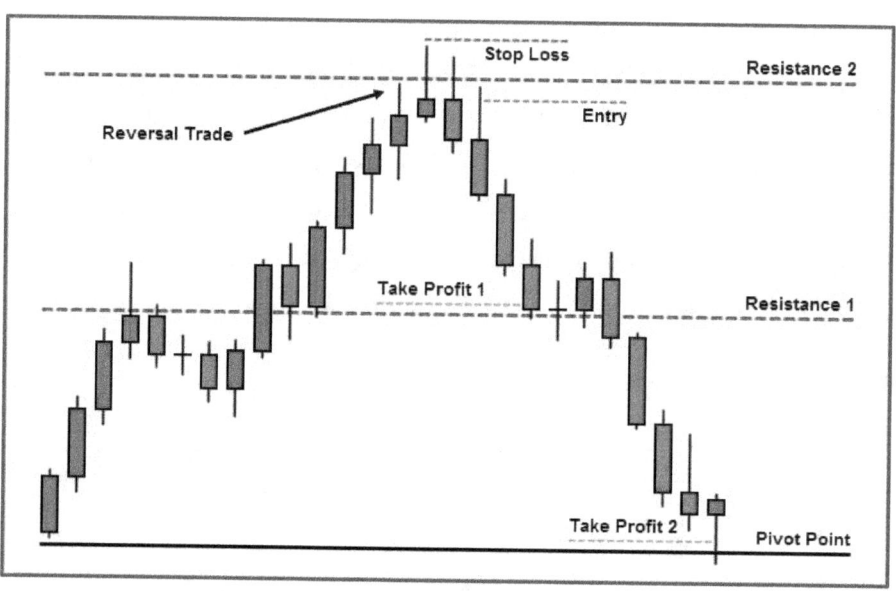

Pivot Point in the Forex Market

The Forex market is open 24 hours every day during the week. The authority forex exchanging day starts and finishes at 5:00 pm Eastern Standard Time (EST) toward the finish of the US exchanging meeting. Pivot points are determined in light of the ups and downs of the whole 24-hour time frame, and the nearby toward the finish of the American session is utilized in most pivot point mini-computers. At times levels are not generally applicable for traders who just exchange during the London or American session. They exchange just a little piece of the day, however utilize a pointer in view of 24-hour price development.

Pivot point can likewise be applied in view of four hour or hourly highs, lows and closing prices. Traders can also add Pivot points to their cost chart and change the indicators time span. This will give more expected regions to perception over a day time span. During this day time span, six different set of control points are created. This can give more possible exchanges or better comprehension, specifically for 26hours forex traders.

Trading Using Pivot Points

If we can recall earlier, the pivot point is an average an average of the high, low and closing prices from the past trading day.

Now the pivot point can be utilized in two ways.

- The pivot point can be used in determining the general trend of the market. In the event that the price of the pivot point breaks out in a vertical development, then, at that point, the market is bullish. On the off chance that the cost falls beneath the pivot point, then it tell us that it is a bearish movement.

- They are also utilized to enter and leave the market.

The outcome of the pivot point framework relies upon the merchant and his capacity to involve in relation to different types of technical analysis. Other technical pointers can be; MACD to candle patterns. The more prominent the quantity of positive signs of a trade, the more noteworthy the odds of coming out on profitably.

Calculating Pivot Points

The pivot point indicators can be added to an outline and it will consequently make levels and show it. Remember that Pivot points are determined from highs, lows and closing price from the previous day.(yesterday)

So on the off chance that you needs to make Pivot points levels for the present day, you would have to do it this way

$P = (H + L + C)/3$

Pivot Point = (Previous High + Previous Low + Previous Close) / 3

$R1 = (P \times 2) - L$

$S1 = (P \times 2) - H$

$R2 = P + (H - L) = P + (R1 - S1)$

$S2 = P - (H - L) = P - (R1 - S1)$

where:

R1 - Resistance Level 1

P - Pivot Point

L - Previous Low

S1 - Support Level 1

R2 - Resistance Level 2

S2 - Support Level 2

H - Previous High

- High indicates - the highest price from the prior trading day,
- Low indicates - the lowest price from the prior trading day,
- Close indicates - the closing price from the prior trading day.
- Sum the high, low, and close and then divide by three.
- Mark the prize as P on the chart
- When P (price) is known, traders would need to calculate Support1 and support 2 as well as resistance1 and resistance 2.

The pivot point calculation is important to set the levels of stops, entry and take profit.

Frequently Asked Questions

What is a pivot Point Level?

In this kind of exchanging, In the event that the analysis of the previous day is over the pivot point, the market is supposed to follow a bullish nature.

Then again if the opposite is the case and the analysis of the previous day is beneath the pivot point, the market is supposed to follow a bearish nature.

How many pivot levels are there?

There are seven pivot levels on the chart where the basic pivot level lies in the center of the chart and three of the support pivot levels lie over the basic pivot, and three of the resistance pivot levels lie beneath the basic pivot.

What is a pivot bounce?

The pivot bounce is one of the significant strategies, and it guides the trader when to purchase the stock and when to sell them. The focal point of this technique is to find the bounce in prices at Pivot points in the charts.

What is a pivot breakout?

In this procedure, the short exchange is performed when the pattern shows a bearish exhibition and has a long position when the pattern shows a bullish presentation.

Momentum Trading Strategy

In momentum trading we buy low and sell high. It seems to be a clear response to a market change. Yet, it can't be simply simple. How about we make a plunge and figure out how it tends to be utilized and when, also what are the best types of indicators, to comprehend, when it is best utilized.

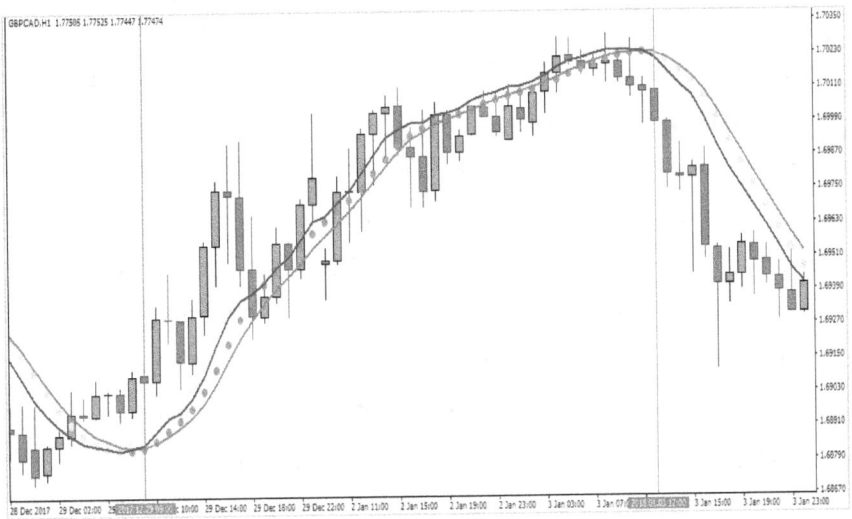

This strategy wasn't that famous until Richard Driehaus gave the general tour: he utilized it to run his assets and succeeded. The thought was that with "purchasing high and selling higher" strategy more cash could be made. He accepted that selling washout stocks and purchasing champs is a functioning methodology. Later on procedures he utilized summarized the momentum strategy.

This strategy is set to take advantage of market instability; taking short term positions on stocks that are going up and holding on until they begin giving indications of falling and selling them. Furthermore, along the chain goes, tracking down champs and getting them and selling the washouts.
The momentum financial investor looks to exploit the crowd intuition of investors by driving the group and being quick to remove the cash and flee.

Day Trading Momentum Strategies
The market needs to move, in day trading to enable one make money based on market fluctuation. Now momentum trading in regards to day trading fits in properly.

So how do one track down the right stock and take action - purchase low, sell high?

As a matter of some importance, traders need to find a stock that is moving. We are not interested in stock that doesn't move.

The whole point of day trading is to enter and leave numerous positions rapidly over the course of the day, fully intent on creating a gain from little cost developments. With that in mind momentum traders search for markets and stocks with a high volume, so they can trade stocks rapidly without interference. At the point when a range is no less than $5, it is viewed as profitable for . momentum daily traders. Lesser price movement are more profitable for scalping strategies, which are exceptionally normal inside the forex market.

Momentum trading is a strategy where traders purchase assets once they have been influenced by current cost trends. Brokers will generally exploit upswings or downtrends in monetary markets until the trends starts to disappear.

This strategies centers around price developments, a type of specialized analysis that is extremely famous with short term traders. Here traders calculate momentum price in light of authentic value trends and information, and given the unpredictability of monetary markets, prices can move and the market can move in unforeseen bearings unexpectedly.

We should not fail to remember that press releases impacts the market as well as other macroeconomic occasions, all these should be put into consideration.

Preferable Momentum Indicators

Technical analysis tools that assistance to distinguish the strength or the weakness of the stock's cost are momentum indicators. The 3 common momentum indicators are listed below:
1. Relative Strength Index (RSI)
2. Moving Average Convergence Divergence (MACD)

3. Average Direction Index (ADX).

The Relative Strength Index is quite possibly the most famous momentum indicators. Likewise an oscillator, the RSI acts like a measurement for price changes as well as the speed at which they change. The Relative Strength Index fluctuates to and fro somewhere in the range of Zero to 100. At the point when the relative strength index values are transcending 50, the sign is positive upturn momentum, however, when the relative strength index reaches 70 or over, it's a sign of overbought conditions. Also, the other way around, relative strength index readings that falls under 50 show negative, downtrend momentum. On the off chance that relative strength index readings are under 30, it signifies oversold conditions possibly.

The Moving Average Convergence Divergence is another famous indicators; shows momentum as it wavers between moving average as they converge, cross-over, and get away from each other. A significant part of the MACD is the histogram, which uncovers the contrast between the Moving Average Convergence Divergence line and the 9 day Exponential Moving Average. At the point when the histogram is positive over the zero midpoint line yet starts to fall towards the midline, and that implies debilitating uptrend. On the opposite side, if the histogram is negative, under the zero midpoint line however starts to move towards it, it flags that the downtrend is debilitating.

Average directional index is utilized to gauge when a trend is picking up or losing momentum. It is determined in light of a moving average of price activity throughout some stretch of time, and displayed as a solitary line on the chart. When an average directional index value is 25 or over is a sign of a solid trend, and when a value is under 25 is viewed as a powerless trend and momentum turn traders will normally try not to utilize techniques inside this range. The higher tops on a graph show that a pattern energy is rising, though more smaller peaks imply that force is entering a downtrend, and that implies that a trader ought to leave his/her position.

Momentum Indicators are significant apparatuses for traders, yet they are seldom utilized in disengagement. It is more commonsense to utilize them with other technical indicator that uncovers trend directions. When a direction has been determined, these indicators are important on the grounds that they indicate the strength of price development trends and when they are reaching to the end.

It is wise to note that Momentum trading isn't ideal for everybody - it is dangerous and requires proficient touch, yet it has its prizes, frequently prompts enormous profits. One needs to be very disciplined to trade this kind of style since trade must be closed at the earliest hint of weakness and the assets should be promptly positioned into an alternate trade that is displaying strength. Purchasing high and selling higher is the primary objective, however this objective doesn't come without its reasonable portion of difficulties and dangers.

Carry Trade Strategy

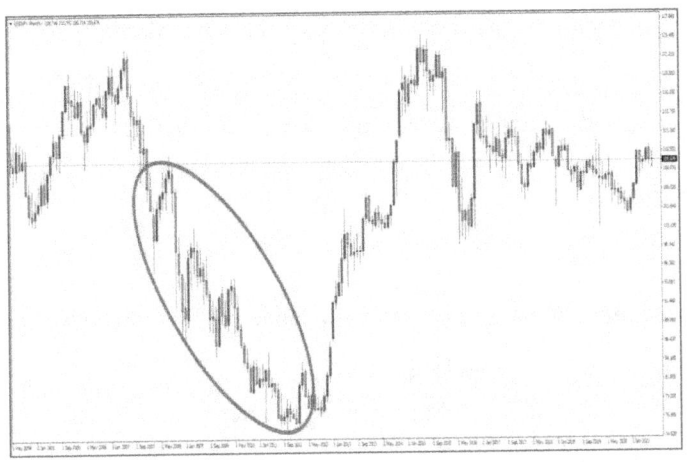

The carry trade strategy is a strategy which involves getting loan at a low interest rate and investing it into a resource with a higher interest rate. As a matter fact of facts carry trade is based sometimes on borrowing in a currency with low interest rate and then converting these currencies that was borrowed into another currency with a high interest rate. This strategy can be utilized on stocks, commodities, land and securities that are denominated in the subsequent currency.

For Instance

Assuming a trader acquires 1000 japanese Yen with 0 interest rate, then, at that point, converts the Yen to Us Dollar, and goes ahead to buy US bonds with 10,6 percent interest. This investors will create a gain of 10,6%, as long as the conversion rate between US dollar and Yen remains the same

Numerous investors utilizes this strategy , since it's easy, straightforward and profitable particularly when leverage is utilized, on the off chance that the trade referenced above had a leverage of 10:1, the trader would create 106% gain. However, the greater potential profit the greater is the risk, assuming that by any chance the conversion rate between US dollar and Yen change, lets say that the US dollar falls in relation to Yen, the trade will lose value and the trade will be at huge loss. Once leverage is involved and the swapping rate changes, traders will lose 10 times more worth (in the event that the trader doesn't hedge properly).

Just like all other strategy, the carry trade strategy also has its strength and weaknesses

Weakness

- The present risk of rapid decrease in currencies conversion rate, which will most likely reduce the profits to nothing.
- Just like an invested asset, there could be change in price which would in return drop the worth of the income.

Strength

- The most appealing sides of carry trade strategy is its effortlessness.
- Ability to allows traders make use of leverage

In the event that a trader chooses to utilize this strategy, it's very important to have the expertise and always be on the look out if any changes are to occur.

Risk Management Control

There is no question that Forex exchanging procedure is very succulent yet has a considerable lot of risk, to clean this methodology utilizing risk management is encouraged. Without this, traders account can be blown by an unforeseen event. To be successful in carry trading always enter trades when fundamentals and market sentiment support them.

The most awful time to utilize Carry Trading strategy is during the time of interest rate decrease. Change in financial policy likewise implies an adjustment of currency values. If rates drops, demand for the money will in general drop too.

In summary Carry Trading Strategy is beneficial, particularly when leverage is utilized, very basic and unsafe. For traders to be profitable, they need to know the perfect time to get in and out of a carry trade. Also, it is very vital that before one should use this risky strategy you must have the ability and the skill alongside experience.

Hedging Strategy

The main reason of hedging is to decrease risk to a minimal level.

In the forex market the most common process of safeguarding a position in a cash pair from the risk of losing money is called hedging.

Forex Hedging strategy is a type of momentary protection when a trader is worried about information or events setting off unpredictability in money markets.

Presently there are numerous hedging methodologies out there however we would be categorizing them into three:

- Direct hedging
- Correlation hedging
- Hedging with options

Direct hedging

This is the point at which when a trader currently has a position on a money pair, and opens the contrary position on the exact paring.

For instance, in the event that a trader is long on **EUR/USD**, now that trader will open a short position with the exact trade size.

This will prompt a net benefit or deficiency of nothing, contingent upon the expenses of opening each trade. Numerous traders would just close off the initial position and acknowledge loss. But a trader that hedged directly would bring in cash with the second trade that would forestall this misfortune.

Correlation Hedging

Correlation Hedging is the point at which a trader is searching for a correlation between multiple currency pairs. This is done by choosing two currencies that basically have a positive relationship, move in a similar direction and afterward taking opposing positions on selected currency pairs..

For instance: on the off chance that a trader is holding long on **EUR/USD**, they can support with a short situation on **GBP/USD**.

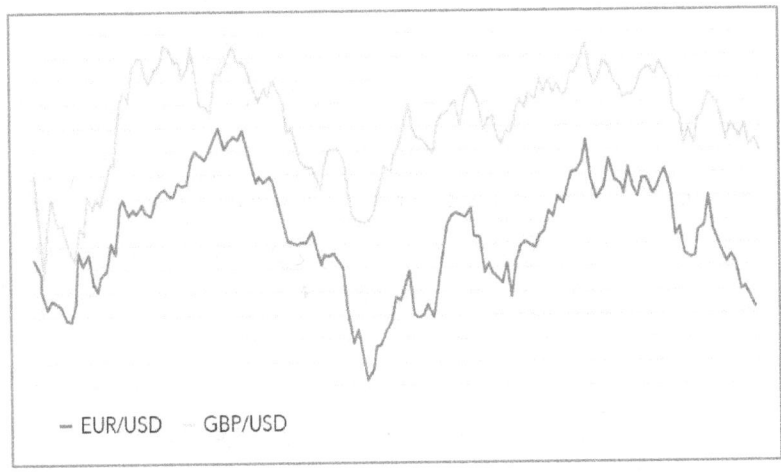

Once a trader utilize a correlation hedging strategye, it is critical to recollect that their risk is presently spreading on different currencies. Even though positive correlation works when economies are moving in union, any slight deviation can influence the movement of each currency pair and correspondingly the traders hedging.

Hedging with options

Now to safeguard ones position from market volatility, a trader can purchase put or call options based upon the direction of their trading. Options can be seen as momentary insurance contract and, in that capacity, accommodate the installment of an insurance premium. Putting to the fact that the trader pays this premium whether or not they close or holds their positions.

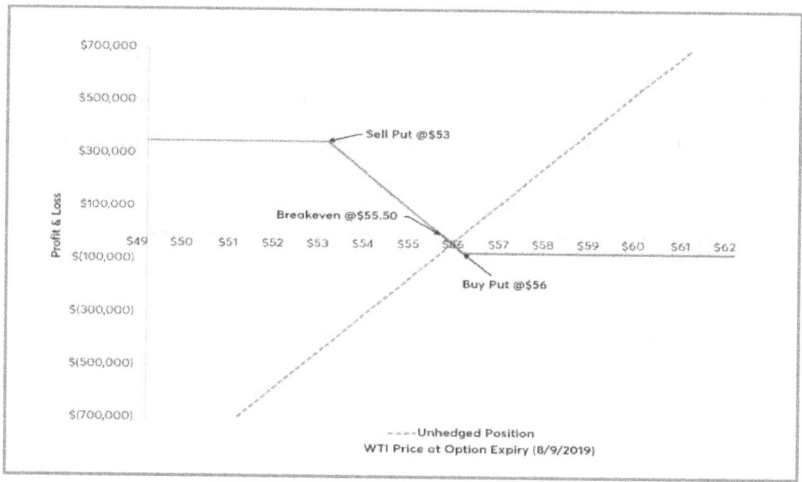

Practically speaking, suppose a trader purchased a put option when he had a long position on a currency pair, however there were worries that impacting elements could prompt a fall in the worth of the pair. A put option permits the trader to set the strike cost and termination date for the sale to be made at that strike cost.

On the off chance that the worth fell, the traders misfortunes would be restricted to the worth of the premium payable to the option seller, in addition to the distinction between the strike cost and the cost of the money pair at the time the put was bought.

Hedging Currency Risks

Currency risk can quickly spoil profits, particularly when the market is unpredictable. Thus, traders who put themselves in an unsafe circumstance in unfamiliar market: it could be traditional investments, land deals, commercial purchases, it is important to consider the money risk. Some traders might feel alright with the risk of conversion rate volatility and will attempt to exploit it. Others might on the other hand like to keep away from such vulnerability. Anyway, traders need to consider the dangers related with currency exchange so as not to risk their cash.

To begin hedging risks, below are a couple of steps each trader ought to do.

- Traders must have an unmistakable comprehension of their monetary objectives and goals
- They ought to distinguish where Forex openings are, and what that might mean for their goals
- Perform pressure test and some situation examinations
- Check in with their tolerance to risk
- While picking a hedging style and strategy, they ought to think about agreeable levels of risk and monetary objectives
- Traders ought to follow, assess and adjust their hedging style as situations arises

In a Nutshell

Hedging involves money spending, it's like protection. Forex hedging strategy is an extraordinary method for limiting openness to risk. It assists traders with safeguarding against potential losses, likewise it can assist with creating a gain. New traders to the foreign conversion market ought to proceed cautiously, and never risk more than they can stand to lose, so utilizing hedging methodologies is a good beginning for novices.

Fledgling or not, Hedging is intricate and requires skill, to appropriately execute it. Traders should develop confidence in conjecturing on market swings, and recognize factors that has the probability to impact the market.

Basket Trading Strategy

Broadening is a brilliant rule in exchanging, which is the premise of basket trading strategy. In a nutshell, don't tie up your resources in one basket.

Basket trading in Forex is selling and purchasing different money pairs at the same time, they can be both related or uncorrelated. It can also be used on different financial markets, like Forex, stock, futures, etc. The objective is to exit in excess after closing off every open position. That is, few out of every position should be won, yet the total should be positive.

This strategy allows a trader to make a rundown of stocks, called a basket, that they can save, exchange, manage and follow as one entity. Baskets can be utilized to put resources into and track stocks assembled by investment style, market area, life event, or any characterization a trader picks.

Basket Trading Example

Right off the bat, traders ought to find a specific currency pair that has an unmistakable trend, bullish or bearish. In the wake of deciding the overall direction of a specific cash pair in light of the strength and weaknesses of the two currencies, a basket of currencies can then chosen.

For instance, in the event that a trader has established a strong GBP/USD bearish trend, it will end up being the base Forex pair for their basket. GBP/USD bearish trend implies that the **United States dollar** is fortifying.

Having established that Dollar is getting strong, rather than going short just for GBP/USD pair, traders ought to expand and likewise go short for AUD/USD, EUR/USD and CAD/USD.

Now if that trader wanted to risk 4% just for GBP/USD trade, this risk can be disseminated on each of the four currency pairs. 1% GBP/USD, 1% CAD/USD,

1% AUD/USD and 1% EUR/USD exclusively. Obviously, assuming the main trend isn't established correctly, losses are unavoidable.

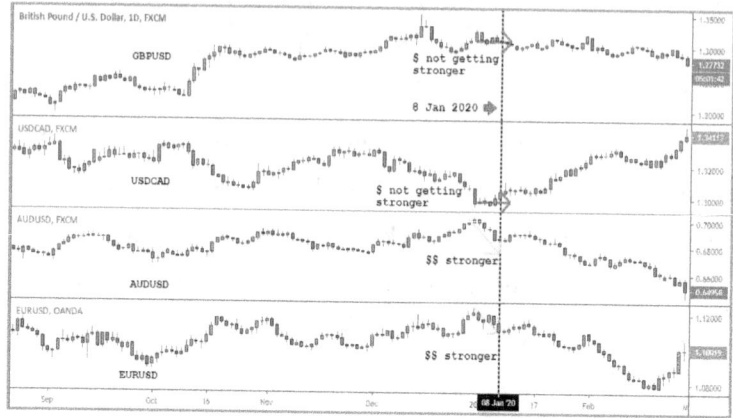

Advantages Basket trading

- Assists investors with controlling their investment. Traders can add or eliminate individual or a few securities to the basket.
- Basket strategy make it simple for investors to scatter their investment across numerous securities.
- Investors can make a basket that matches their investment objectives. Basket may contain stocks from a particular area or stocks with a particular market cap.

Basket trading strategy hardly have hindrances, the entire reason for it is to diversify the risk. Gains include: customized decision, simple circulation and control.

Losing trades is a vital piece of basket trading too, and traders ought to be ready for it while making a portfolio. While utilizing this technique it is vital to have in portfolio resources that will balance those losses in order to come out with a profit.

If done carefully, this strategy has the potential for a major measure of profits.

Buy and Hold Strategy

The buy and hold strategy in a long term investment strategy, it involves a trader purchasing stocks, currency pairs or different kinds of securities, for example, ETFs and holds them for a long stretch of time, paying little mind to transient fluctuations int the market. The thought behind purchase and hold strategy is based on long haul tendencies.

This strategy is one of the most well known and proven ways of putting resources into the financial market. Investors don't have to stress over timing the market or going with choices in view of emotional models and analysis.

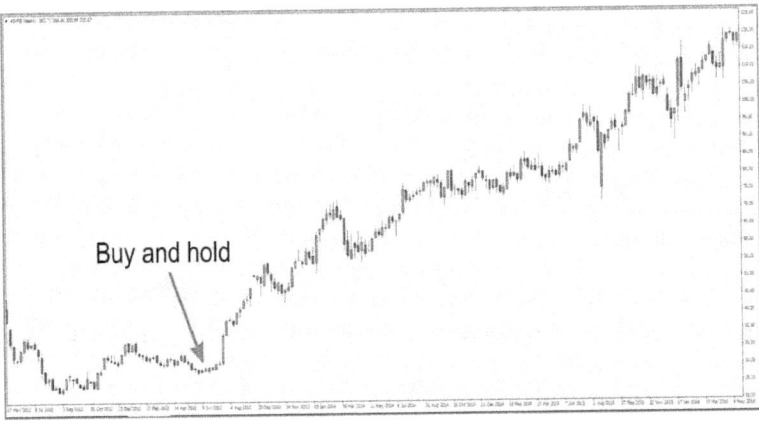

How Does the Buy and Hold Strategy Work

At the point when an investor purchase stocks, deduced turns into the partial proprietor of the company with honors that include casting a ballot rights and a stake for corporate benefits as the company develops. Assuming that how much shares purchased is significant, investors can impact and guarantee their future benefit. Investors vote on basic issues, like consolidations and acquisitions, and choose chiefs for the board.

Traders need to comprehend and acknowledge that change requires time. Rather than treating stocks just as a momentary benefit, similar to day traders, traders ought to invest long haul through high points and low points.

Advantages of Buy and Hold Strategy
- Purchase and hold strategy has demonstrated endlessly time again to produce significant returns on investment. Warren Buffett, Peter Lynch, Jack Bogle, John Templeton, and Benjamin Graham to mention but a few, are titans of purchase and hold strategy, their experience demonstrate how well this strategy can function. Obviously, expertise of stock picking is the fundamental justification for success.

- Traders can pause for a moment or two and visualize the overall qualities of the market, the assets and the open doors for future development, and just let the investment do its thing without stressing over attempting to see as the "great" entries and exits or continually looking at prices.

Disadvantages of Buy and Hold Strategy
- Once a trader purchase and is holding a stock means they are held up in that investment for the lengthy timespan. Thus traders must have the self control to not pursue other investment importunity during this holding time frame. This is challenging to practice, when purchased stock is lagging.

- There is no particular time span after which stock will begin developing, therefore traders need to equip themselves with perseverance.

- Based on the fact that a stock has been held for a long time, doesn't imply that it is dependable. In the event that or when an emergency occurs, everything could turn into loss.

The purchase and hold strategy is a long term investment strategy that is ideal for traders who lack time and to continue to follow up with their investment portfolio on a daily basis. Implementation of the strategy all alone isn't hard, however traders must have the intellect to find a growing or underestimated stock.

Pair/Spread Trading Strategy

The pair trading strategy is a unique trading strategy that has to do with matching a long position with a short position in two stocks with high connection. This strategy depends on the verifiable correlation of two stocks. The stocks in a pair exchange should have a high sure correlation, which is the main thrust behind the technique's benefits.

This trading trading strategy is best utilized when a trader recognizes a relationship divergence. In view of the verifiable conviction that two securities will keep a specific correlation, should be utilized when correlation vacillates. Profits are conceivable when failing stock recovers value and the price of a more excellent security falls. The net benefit is the total gain acquired from the two positions.

The pair trading strategy works with options, currencies, commodities and even stocks.

What is Spread Trading

Spread trading is the process of buying one security and selling another related security as a unit. This strategy are normally utilized futures contracts or options, to get a general net exchange with a positive worth called the spread. Spread Exchanging is done in pairs so it disposes execution risk.

Advantages of Spread Exchanging

- Trades generally last 6 - 21 days, and that implies, capital is consistently working for a trader.
- Spread trading gives chances to consistent pay.
- It's an ideal technique to utilize when the market is unpredictable.
- Spread trading offers a lower risk opportunity.

☐☐

Disadvantage of Spread Trading

- Profits are very lower.

- It is not difficult to overdo it and start to trade emotionally. Do not forget to minimize your losses and utilize logic to trade not emotions

Types of Spread Trades

- Option spreads
- Interest rate swap spreads
- Intracommodity (Calendar) spreads
- Intercommodity spreads

Option spreads

Option spread are formed with various options agreements on a similar or the same basic commodity or stock.

Interest rate swap spreads

These are type of spreads that are formed with **LEGS** in various currencies but the equivalent or comparative maturities.

Inter-commodity spreads

These are spreads that are formed from two unmistakable but related commodities, mirroring the monetary connection between them.

Intra-commodity or Calendar spreads

This is a type of spread trading that is based on simultaneously buying futures or options lapsing on a specific date and the sale of a similar or the same instrument lapsing on another date. These singular buys, known as the **LEGS** of the spread, fluctuate just in expiration date; they depend on a similar fundamental market and strike price.

Calendar Spread Options

This is an option strategy that comprises of purchasing and selling two options of same type and strike price, yet unique termination cycles.

There are Vertical and Inclining spreads.

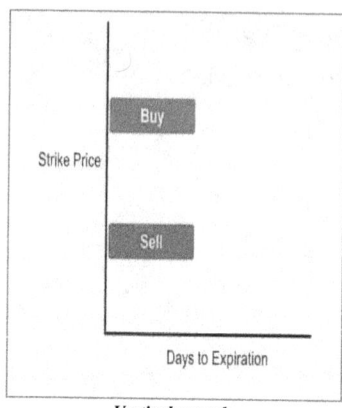

Vertical spread

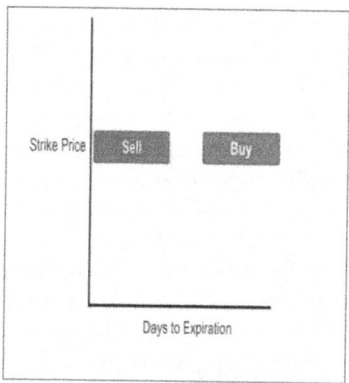

Diagonal spread

Calender spread is a future or option strategy that happens by simultaneously opening a long and a short position on a similar fundamental asset, yet with various delivery dates. In a common calender spread, traders would purchase a more long term contract and go short a closer term option with the same strike cost. On the off chance that two different strike costs are utilized for every month, this is known as a diagonal spread.

The common calender spread trade is based on the sale of an option (either a put or call) with a close term lapse date and the concurrent acquisition of an option (put or call) with a more extended term expiration. The two options are of a similar types and commonly utilize a same strike price. Furthermore, there is a reverse calender spread which involves a trader taking the contrary position;

purchasing a short term option e and selling a more long term option on the same or a similar underlying security.

Calendar Spread Options Illustration

XYZ stock is trading at $146.05 in late March, a trader can go into the accompanying calender spread:

Sell the May 146 call for $0.97 ($97 for one agreement)

Purchase the June 73 call for $1.27 ($107 for one agreement)

The net expense (charge) of the spread accordingly is (1.09 - 0.97) $0.12 (or $12 for one spread).

This above calender spread will pay off the most assuming XYZ shares remain generally level until the May options lapse, permitting the trader to gather the premium for the option that was sold. Then, at that point, in the event that the stock moves up between then and June expiry, the subsequent leg will profit.

Now the ideal market move for benefit would depend on the price turn out to be more volatile in the close term, yet to generally rise, shutting just under 140 as of the May lapse. This permits the May option agreement to lapse yet permit the trader to benefit from up moves until the may expiration.

Swing Trading Strategy

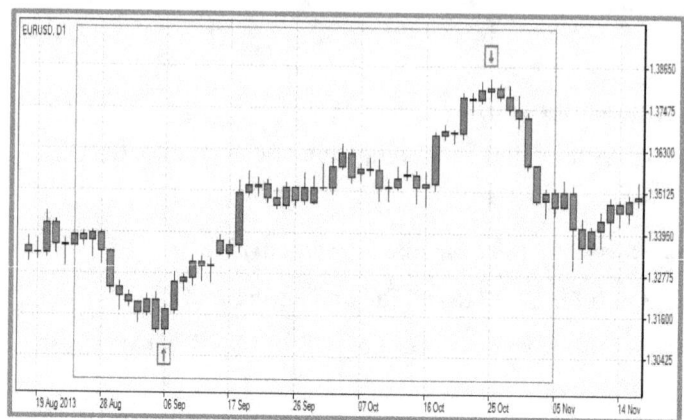

Swing trading is a drawn out exchanging procedure, when trades are kept open from a couple of days to half months. Swing exchanging system's essence is exploiting market enormous fluctuations "swings". Fundamental analysis assumes a significant part on longer time spans.

Solid directional moves are in many cases set off by significant or surprising business sector news, for example, corporate pay proclamations or national bank gatherings, and that implies swing traders should know about market basics. There are ways of fostering a dependable trading plan. However swing exchanging is to a greater degree a drawn out strategy, it can also be utilized on the day to day chart too.

Positive sides
- Traders utilizing this strategy need less time to exchange than day trading.
- Improves the trading system, since traders can depend just on technical analysis.

Negative sides
- Since traders use swing exchanging on everyday charts they may frequently miss the more extended term trends for transient market moves.

- Sharp market inversions can prompt critical losses.

Swing trading includes taking exchanges that can endure from two or three days to a while to benefit from the normal cost development. The objective of swing exchanging is to discover a portion of the potential cost development. A few trader might be searching for unstable stocks with clear large moves, while others might lean toward calmer stocks. In the two cases, swing exchanging is the most common way of figuring out where the stock cost can move straightaway, entering a position and afterward creating a gain assuming that that move happens.

There are ways of fostering a solid trading plan. Below are the most well-known technical indicators that can be utilized to assist with creating swing trading techniques that will work.

Moving average crossovers
When the more limited term moving average crosses over the more extended term moving average, it's a purchase signal, as it shows that the trend is moving up. This is known as a "brilliant cross."

Cup-and-handle patterns
This is a technical chart design that looks like a cup and handle where the cup is looking like a "u" and the handle has a slight descending float. A cup and handle is viewed as a bullish sign broadening an uptrend, and is utilized to detect valuable chances to go long.

Head and shoulders patterns
This is a technical indicator that has a chart pattern portrayed by three pinnacles, the external two are close in height and the center is most elevated. A head and shoulders design portrays a particular chart development that predicts a bullish to bearish reversal pattern.

Flags

This areas of tight union in price activity showing a counter pattern move that trails behind a sharp directional development in price. The pattern normally comprises of somewhere in the range of five and twenty cost bars. These pattern can be either up or descending trending (bullish or bearish flag)

Triangles

A triangle is a graph design, portrayed by drawing trendlines along a uniting cost range, that implies a respite in the overall pattern. Specialized analysts classify triangles as continuation patterns.

Swing trading is really one of the most incredible trading styles since it offers huge benefit potential for traders. Swing traders get feedback on their trade following two or three days which is a valid statement to keep them on toes and inspired.

The swing trading can be said to be the in the centre between trend trading and day trading.

Trading Order Types Strategy

Its important to carry out or test a trading order strategy before any trader begins to trade stocks. Furthermore, in other for that trader must have a comprehension of what kind of order in which cases to utilize.

Contingent upon exchanging style, various sorts of orders can be utilized to actually stocks more efficiently. Orders assist traders with effective money management style.

A stock order is a bunch of guidelines traders sends off to a brokerage to purchase or sell securities. Underneath are types of order, so you would be equipped and prepared to involve it in your effective money management strategy.

Forex Order Types

1. Take Profit
2. Good 'Til Canceled
3. Day Order
4. Market Order
5. All Or None
6. Quick Or Drop (Immediate Or Cancel)
7. Fill Or Kill
8. Stop Loss Order
9. Stop Limit Order
10. Limit Order

Take Profit

Take Profit is constantly associated with a vacant position of a forthcoming order and planned to close off the trade at a profit when it has reached at a specific level. In some cases trader refer to this order as target profit.

Good 'Til Canceled

Here the order will remain active until the trader chooses to cancel it, unquestionably brokerage organizations set a period cap for this kind of order but it wont go beyond 3 months.

Day Order

For instance if a trader don't specifically set a time frame of expiry by giving instructions, the order will automatically be set as a day order. The trader will have to enter the transaction afresh because at the end of a trading day the order will lapse.

Market Order

This is the most straightforward type of trade because it is an order to purchase or sell promptly at the current cost. A very significant thing to recollect is that the last traded cost isn't really the price at which the market request will be executed. In unstable markets, the cost at which traders execute the exchange can contrast from the last exchanged cost. The cost will continue as before just when the bid/ask cost is precisely at the last traded cost.

Always remember market orders ensure the request's prompt execution, however don't ensure a price.

All or None

This kind of order is particularly significant for those purchasing cheap stocks. A go big or go home ordering guarantees that the trader will either get the whole measure of the mentioned amount of stock or not get it by any means. This is tricky when the stock is very iliquid or there is a breaking point on the order.

For instance, assuming you put in an order to purchase 4,000 XYZ shares, yet just 2,000 are sold, the go big or go home cutoff implies that the traders order won't be executed until somewhere around 4,000 offers are accessible at the favored price. In the event that the trader doesn't put a go big or go home limit, the order for 4,000 shares will be to some extent filled for 2,000 shares.

Quick or Drop (Immediate or Cancel)

This is any order sum that could be executed in the market in an exceptionally brief timeframe, most frequently in a few seconds or less, would be filled, then the remainder of the order would be dropped. Assuming no shares are traded during this "quick" stretch, the order is totally dropped.

Fill or Kill

This is a blend of All Or None order with Immediate Or Cancel particular, the thought behind is that the whole order size to be traded in an exceptionally brief timeframe (a couple of seconds), on the off chance that conditions aren't met the order we be totally canceled or dropped.

Stop Loss Order

This is one of the main type of orders where a trader can restrict his misfortunes by leaving a trade in the event that a particular price is reached. While placing a stop loss order, traders can shield themselves from causing high misfortunes in the event that the price conflicts with them. At the point when a trader puts in a purchase order, he is anticipating that the price should go up, so he can procure a profit. And yet the price could go down, so to keep away from misfortunes the trader submits a stop loss order at a price underneath the purchase price.

For instance

This is a buy order of a trader

Share price = Rs. 400

Stop loss at Rs. 396

The trader anticipates that the share price should go higher, to procure a profit. In the event that the cost falls beneath Rs. 400, say it tumbles to Rs. 390.

The trader will have a deficiency of Rs. 4 for each offer (400 - 396) and leave the trade. But the trader didn't put a stop loss, the misfortune would have been Rs (400-390) = Rs 10 for each share, which is more prominent than the above situation.

Likewise, when a trader submits an offer request, he anticipates that the price should fall, so he can procure a profit. In any case, it might happen that rather than the price going down, the price goes up. So to stay away from high misfortunes when price go down, merchant can put a stop-misfortune at a price higher than the selling price.

On the off chance that a trader has put in a purchase order at Rs. 400, he can put a stop-misfortune cost at Rs. 390. In the event that the cost goes down, he will book a deficiency of Rs. 10 for each share and leave the trade

Stop Limit Order

This is a unique limit order that has 2 prices, (a) is the stop price, which changes over the order into a sell order, (b) is the limit or cutoff price. Rather than turning into a market sell order, a sell order turns into a cutoff order that will just execute at the cutoff price or better. This can relieve a likely issue with stop misfortune orders, which can be set off during an unexpected accident when costs fall but recuperate.

Limit order

This order some of the time alluded to as a forthcoming order, it is a sort of request that permits trader to trade a security at a specific cost in the future. A trader can set the price in a limit order but this is impossible in a market order where the trader has zero command over price.

Limit order can be utilized during high unpredictability; it assists with controlling the cost at which we trade a security. Limit order is helpful when trader are not effectively following the price development of a stock and need to trade at a foreordained price. Below are are 4 sorts of limit order

1. Buy Limit
2. Sell Limit
3. Buy Stop
4. Sell Stop

Buy limit: this is a order to purchase a security at a predefined price or below. Limit orders should be put on the right half of the market to guarantee that they take care of business when the cost rises. For a limit purchase order, this implies placing a request at or underneath the current market price.

Sell Limit: This is an order to sell a security at or over a predetermined cost. To guarantee a superior value, the order should be set at or over the ongoing market ask.

Buy Stop: This an order to purchase a security at a price over the ongoing market bid. The stop order to purchase becomes dynamic solely after a predetermined cost level has been reached; known as the stop level. Purchase stop orders are set over the market and sell stop orders set underneath the market. When a stop level has been reached, the order will be promptly changed over into a market or limit order.

Sell Stop: this is an order to sell a security at a cost lower the ongoing market ask. Like the purchase stop, a stop request to sell becomes active solely after a predefined cost level has been reached.

Buy Limit versus Sell Stop Order

Expert traders commonly use trade orders for their trades, however it doesn't prevent them from slippage. Slippage means the distinction between the normal price of a trade and the price at where that trade is executed. Brokerage organizations offer more developed sorts of orders that permit determine sell and buy prices, which can assist with keeping a trader from losing a lot of money.

In a nutshell, advanced orders kill slippage and guarantee that trades are executed at the right price if or when the market cost is reached.

Earlier I listed various kinds of orders utilized in trading, below I will be listing out the contrasts between generally utilized **ODERS BUY LIMIT and SELL STOP ORDER.**

A limit order sets the predefined price for the order and executes the trade at that predefined price.	A purchase limit order will be executed at or underneath the limit price.
A limit sell order will be executed at the cutoff price or higher.	A limit order permits traders to determine a price.
A stop order incorporates a particular boundary for setting off a trade. When the stock cost reach the stop price, l v vt will be executed at the following accessible market cost.	Subsequently, a purchase stop ought to typically incorporate a price over the ongoing market price, and a sell stop ought to incorporate a price beneath the ongoing market price.
A stop order is typically doled out for edge trading or supporting purposes as it for the most part has limitations on the best way to enter the price.	☐A purchase stop order will be executed at the next accessible market price after the purchase stop price boundary is reached.
A sell stop will be executed at the next accessible market price after the sell stop has been reached.	Purchase stops are typically used to close a short position in a stock, while sell stops are normally utilized for stop losses.

Traders need to realize the distinction among limit and market order. Contingent upon the circumstance some will be a more reasonable methodology. A long term trader is bound to pick a market order in light of the fact that the choice depends on crucial rules that could keep going for a really long time, so the ongoing market sector cost isn't an issue.

The trader, in any case, will in general act based on the momentary trend on the chart and is in this way significantly more mindful of the market price paid; a limit order to purchase in with a stop loss order to sell is typically the absolute minimum for setting up an exchange.

At the point when traders understand what each order does and how every one could affect trading, they can distinguish which order suits their venture needs, that does not take much time, more significantly decreases dangers saves cash.

Algorithmic Trading Strategies

This is a technique for order execution utilizing pre customized programmed trading guidelines, considering factors like time, price and volume.

In the trading scene algorithmic trading is additionally called algo trading, mechanized exchanging. It is a PC program that adheres to a bunch of directions for setting an trading. This kind of trading can be productive at a speed and recurrence past the range of a human trader.

Algorithms traders can make large number of exchanges each second, so in the event that a calculation is fixed, it could turn out to be possibly an extremely amazing asset. In 2019 a research showed that around 92% of trading the Forex market was performed by trading algorithms as opposed to people.

A very good and sophisticated algorithm ought to perfectly consider many factors and analysis, like developments of price, market unpredictability, chart analysis and other in any case significant variables. There are numerous methodologies that are broadly utilized for exchanging and they vary extraordinarily in numerous perplexing ways.

Strategies referenced underneath are viewed as Best Algorithmic Strategies.

- Index Fund Rebalancing
- High frequency arbitrage
- Trading Range (Mean Reversion)
- Trend-following Strategies
- Mathematical Model-based Strategies
- Time Weighted Average Price (TWAP)
- Volume-weighted Average Price (VWAP)
- Percentage of Volume (POV)

- Implementation Shortfall

Index Fund Rebalancing
This is a cycle where the basic resources of assets are rearranged by current economic situations. For instance, a pension fund should be a blend of half stocks and half bonds. In a couple of years the worth of stocks increases, and presently compromises 75% of the portfolio. During rebalancing, a portion of the stocks are sold, to carry back the portfolio to the first 50 50 distribution, and the trader benefits. These rebalancing exchanges are presently automatized by calculations.

High frequency arbitrage
Purchasing a double recorded stock at a lower cost in one market and all the while selling it at a greater cost in another market offers the cost differential as hazard free benefit or arbitrage. Same should be possible for stocks versus futures instruments. Carrying out an algorithm to distinguish such cost differentials and submitting the orders productively permits profitable open doors.

Trading Range (Mean Reversion)
This methodology depends on the idea that the high and low prices of an assets are a transitory peculiarity and they will return to their mean worth (normal worth) intermittently. Recognizing and characterizing a price range and carrying out a calculation in light of it permits trades to be put automatically when the cost of an asset breaks all through its characterized range.

Trend following Strategies
Now one of the most widely recognized algorithmic trading techniques to pursue trend in moving averages, channel breakouts, cost level developments, and related specialized indicators . These are the least demanding and most

straightforward techniques to carry out through algorithmic exchanging in light of the fact that these procedures don't include making any expectations or cost forecasts. Exchanging is started when the ideal trend show up, which are simple and easy to execute utilizing algorithms, without going into the intricacy of prescient analysis.

Mathematical Model-based Strategies

Demonstrated numerical models, permit exchanging on a blend of options and the underlying security. Delta unbiased (numerical model) is a portfolio technique comprising of various positions with balancing positive and negative deltas, a proportion contrasting the adjustment of the price of a resource, normally an attractive security, to the relating change in the value of its derivative so the general delta of the resources being referred to sums zero.

Volume weighted Average Price

The point of this procedure is to execute the order near the normal cost between the beginning and end times subsequently limiting market sector influence.

This technique separates a huge order and deliveries more modest lumps of the orders to the market utilizing uniformly partitioned time allotments between a beginning and end time.

Volume-weighted Average Price

The thought behind this methodology is fairly equivalent to the above strategy, volume weighted average price system separates an enormous request and deliveries more modest lumps of the request to the market utilizing stock, explicit verifiable volume profiles. The objective is to execute the order near the volume weighted average price.

Percentage of Volume

Until an exchange order is completely executed, this calculation keeps on sending fractional orders as per a specific support rate and as per the trading volume in the market. This procedure submits orders, in view of the client characterized rate and increases or diminishes this support rate when the stock price arrives at levels the trader has set.

Implementation Shortfall

Here this strategy will likely limit the execution cost of an order by compromising the continuous market, which helps saving money on the expense of the order and profiting from the open door cost of deferred execution. The procedure will expand the designated cooperation rate when the stock cost moves well and decline it when the stock cost moves antagonistically.

Advantages of Algorithmic Trading

The fundamental reasons algorithmic exchanging has become so famous are a direct result of its benefits in speed, precision and lower cost contrasted with manual exchanging.

- Amount of indicators, trading with algorithms has the benefit of examining and executing on various indicators at a speed that no human could do. Trades can be dissected and executed quicker, subsequently more open doors are accessible at better prices.

- Speed is one of the benefits of algo exchanging. Exchanges are being executed naturally and with incredible speed, since they are planted and composed in advance.

- **Capacity to back-test**, with algo exchanging, traders can run the calculations in light of past information to check whether it would've worked previously. It allows the trader to eliminate any defects of an exchanging framework prior to giving it a live shot.

- **Exactness,** a PC automatically executes trades, which precludes human blunder. For example purchasing some unacceptable money pair, or for some unacceptable sum.

- ☐Feelings won't hold up traffic of levelheaded choices, fortunately everything is already robotized and algorithm is the captain.

- ☐Diminished transaction costs, traders don't need to invest such a lot of energy examining and checking markets.

Exchanging Calculations Models

For instance, a broker needs to track down an arbitrage open door, and finds stock that is exchanged on two unique trades with one hour gap between them in addition to stock that is exchanged in various currencies. Here is a legitimate chance of arbitrage. Suppose f.e. Alexion Drugs Inc.Stock , ALXN is recorded in London and New York stock trades. Dealer then will begin searching for arbitrage open doors (in view of contrast in purchase, sell costs in these two trade stages) and begin to shape the algorithm to take advantage of it.

www.ingramcontent.com/pod-product-compliance
Lightning Source LLC
Chambersburg PA
CBHW070319220526
45465CB00004B/1906